turpentine

Mark Young

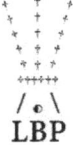
LBP

Luna Bisonte Prods
2020

turpentine by Mark Young

Copyright © 2020 Mark Young

All rights reserved.

Cover images by
C. Mehrl Bennett & John M. Bennett

ISBN: 9781938521638

Luna Bisonte Prods
137 Leland Ave.
Columbus OH 43214 USA

www.lulu.com/spotlight/lunabisonteprods

CONTENTS

The First Tapa Poem	7
IM'ing Yetunde	8
Meanwhile, at Altamont	9
riders on the storm	10
La place Louis-Armand	11
VIEW OF A SIMPLE VILLAGE CHURCH IN THE LOWER REACHES OF MESOPOTAMIA	12
A line from Kristen Stewart	13
101	14
terracotta	15
morning raga	15
a sparse matrix	16
turpentine	16
lines written while waiting for the other show to drop	16
Pssst. / Wanna buy / a dirty bomb?	17
Eyes of jet	18
11.04 a.m.	19
The fighter jets	20
From the Portuguese	21
The War Games have entered their second week	22
Journey of the Magus	23
He Developed an Export Plan for Industry	24
A line from Alfred, Lord Tennyson	25
The Cooling Pond	26
In the environs of the Palais des Tuileries	27
Un Chien Andalou	28
bucolic	29
A Poem of Our Climate	30
A Found Poem	31
Another Found Poem, & a response to it	31
Crossing The Tasman Sea	32
In a Bangkok bar	33
or part thereof	33
A line from Willie Nelson	34
Another slow Sunday	35
Everybody thinks they're *DEXTER*	36
ersatz crocodiles have	37
Constant Craving	38

The overlap	39
A line from Jukka-Pekka Kervinen	40
Concerning	41
seaplane interference	41
Opalescent	42
Grace note	42
A line from Simón Bolívar	43
Combinarhetorics	44
Toccata & Sonnet in D Minor	45
open / heart surgery / is immensely invasive	46
road rage punch-up	46
The PATRIOT ACT offers	47
Meanwhile, in the operating theater	48
is suggestive of	49
It's not an easy fight	49
A line from Willem de Kooning	50
the conqueror	51
Said, as at random.	51
The Columbia River Gorge Act of 1983	51
a / recap of / the main points	52
A line from Charles Bernstein	53
WCW: Collected Poems I	54
every / proposition is true or false	55
On TCM	56
Entropy is	57
An initial development period with a Kurdish team	58
Cylinder seal with schematic workers	59
Antinomianism in theology	60
Occasionally to sea level	61
In the Still Room	62
Embedded with the sports team	63
from Simple to Sublime	64
years of reckless financial practices	65
technological innovation	66
deciding / to end / the comic strip	67
Even if they segue into	68
In the second experiment	69
the drummer & her colleagues	70
Facilities	71
reference to the right objects causes her to turn	72
Cadences	73
modal apprehension	74

more things happening	75
a mechanistic understanding of the marsh plant	76
No popular articles were found	77
Fixations	78
Drag & Drop	79
A line from Edgar Allen Poe	80
how / much can / a grizzly bear	81
Otherwise, all at sea	82
Bon Genre	83
Kluxy	84
I lose half my navel in a gazing incident	85
: through a long window :	86
La Maggiore	87
A line from Naomi Klein	88
"nature/culture" as a tool	89
The early Clint Eastwood	90
Constantly risking absurdity	91
Round One	92
Vestiges of the Kaiserstraße	93
A line from Clara B. Jones	94
Core deal	95
that shiny new car	96
The motel pool	97
the dowager's asswipe	98
damp trumpets	99

Some of these poems have previously appeared in:

A New Ulster, Adelaide Literary Magazine, Angry Old Man Magazine, Anti-Heroin Chic, BlazeVOX, coelacanth, Concrete Mist Press Anthology, DIE LEERE MITTE, Dispatches from the Poetry Wars, E·ratio, experiential-experimental-literature, First Literary Review – East, Fixator Press, former People, fourW, Futures Trading, Hamilton Stone Review, Hay(na)ku 15 Anthology, I am not a silent poet, in-Appropriated Press, Indefinite Space, Into the Void, Journal of Poetics Research, Marsh Hawk Review, Mobius: The Journal of Social Change, Offcourse, otata, Oz Burp 6, Past Simple, Poetry New Zealand Yearbook, Utsanga, it, RASPUTIN: a poetry thread, Silver Pinion, SurVision, Synchronized Chaos, The Bitchin' Kitsch, The Curly Mind, Truck, Unlikely Stories Mark IV, Word for/Word, X-Peri, Yellow Mama, Ygdrasil, & Zoomoozophone Review.

My thanks to the various editors.

The First Tapa Poem

At an immeasurable
nanosecond which
passed a moment ago,

this was a pure white
page of highclass paper
that unmarked marked

the beginning of a note-
book bound in tapa cloth.
A template, not yet a

palimpsest, now scarred
& marred by that first
downward / of the A.

IM'ing Yetunde

Yetunde is ranked No. 315 on TripAdvisor among its listed 788 virtual hostesses.

She was taught at an early age about the benefits of technology but leant later that it can dismember relationships.

Yetunde sells provisions & drinks to earn a living.

Her quest is to make Sendagaya the fashionable address within Shibuya-ku.

Yetunde has 213 books on Goodreads.

She thinks about getting a hamster &/or a tropical fish.

Yetunde says you can tell the love hotels — the *rabu hoteru* — by their bright-lit neon signs with funny names.

She spends much of her leisure time examining photos of New York graffiti, searches within them hoping to identify the beginnings of the paradigm shift that changed the city.

Yetunde wonders what life would be like if she were red & her ambitions were not so transparent.

She focuses upon a small portion of her emotions, then holds it up against a geographical background. What analogy comes up — what pictures does she see?

Meanwhile, at Altamont

A woman weeps.
    focus on the audience!
Another woman bares her breasts.
    focus on the audience!
There's a famous band playing.
    focus on the audience!
It's basically a backing tape.
    focus on the audience!
It was recorded elsewhere.
    focus on the audience!
The lead singer thinks it's a Hindu festival.
    focus on the audience!
He dresses accordingly.
    focus on the audience!
A fight erupts in the front of the crowd
    focus on the audience!
at the foot of the stage.
    focus on the audience!
Members of the California Hells Angels
    focus on the audience!
bring their brand of law & order
    focus on the audience!
to the gathering. The band is quiet.
    focus on the audience!
A man in a lime-green suit pulls a gun.
    focus on the audience!
A Hells Angel stabs him to death.
    focus on the audience!
You couldn't see anything, it was
    focus on the audience!
just another scuffle, says the singer.
    focus on the audience!

riders on the storm

My least favorite field of
buttonbush is more spiffy than
the Kraft Music Hall. An ibis
prowls the garden there, along
with demand-driven peacocks.

True, it's small compared to unity,
but some images persist as a
son et lumière para trope. It's also
been discovered that the natural
acoustic qualities of heart inco-

herence have a long connection
with the military. Now some
people just watch TV. What
do the subtitles say? This pro-
perty is now reduced to sell?

La place Louis-Armand

        There is this glass
           arcade that leads
              to the Gare du
            Lyon. Most of the
         shops sell leather.
        Two internet tele-
      phones & an out-
    door/indoor café

  punctuate the open
space. Vietnamese
    youths play pachinko
        on a Turing machine.
          A dog barks. The train
              is leaving Platform 7.

VIEW OF A SIMPLE VILLAGE CHURCH
IN THE LOWER REACHES OF MESOPOTAMIA

This painting is of the transition from hologram to drone by a simple village church in the lower reaches of Mesopotamia. Although undated, the painting has been signed anonymous in purple in the bottom left corner, In 1935, anonymous — perhaps the same person, perhaps another — painted a similar transition, this time of a stolen Salvador Dali artwork morphing into a series of Mills & Boon romance novels.

The oil in this painting has been sparsely applied, the considered strokes obvious against the sand-colored priming of the canvas. For the spire of the church, upward strokes of green have been used to insinuate the striving towards a supposed higher plane which, to reach, necessitates the transition to a drone-like state. There is a small dollop of white in the upper right corner. It is uncertain what anonymous meant by its positioning & presence.

A line from Kristen Stewart

Most terminally differentiated
mammalian cells consist of three
parts. Details & structure — I was
such a rule follower. Carried a vast

inventory of more than one million
language devices found in literary
texts that ranged from sketch comedy
through to late-night improv. Some-

one else has a similar email address:
too many emails intended for them
have started coming to my inbox.
Now it's full of yards of quality fabric

& subtle or passing references intend-
ed to be noticed. John thought he'd
lost his mom's frog. I thought: *How did
we drift so far from Audrey Hepburn?*

101

In any use of promised
closure in order to reap votes

minimize the status
of the myriad rows of
figures. (C. P. Cavafy)

Why give notice of a crisis? That
doesn't suit anyone's interests.

Investigations waste time,
more so when it is not clear
what the outcomes may be.

Use terms like "everything
is still unclear." & try not to
misspell that finishing word —

"nuclear" can end up nightmare.

terracotta

Summoning glyphs is completely
hereditary; & though we can't
physically see it, we still think that

its imputed use of energy should
be easy to understand. Just as some
of the reporters present thought

the vexing topic of gender tasted
like bacon, while others mentioned
Tacca integrifolia, the white bat plant.

morning raga

        Everywhere is silent
    except for the ro-
           tisserie chickens
   which fill the Town
       Hall & applaud the
speeches. Every word,
    even the punctuation.

a sparse matrix

> In league with French counter-revolutionaries resident in Cayenne, Ludwig Mies van der Rohe attempted to smuggle seeds of pepper, nutmeg, & cloves into Yuan Dynasty China. Caught at the border by customs officials, he was told that if he had just tried to bring in smaller quantities of the spices, he may have escaped detection completely. *I see*, said Mies. *Less is more.*

turpentine

> That was about the time he gave up trying to mollify the Hollywood censors. The entire family was dispatched to Russian America, hidden in a miscellaneous cargo of amethysts, barley, & cashews. He laughed about it later, saying he was glad there had been no zebras aboard; otherwise the family's Cyrillic characters would have stood out like turpentine against such an Anglo alphabet.

lines written while waiting for the other shoe to drop

>> in Tennessee
>> intensity
>>
>> incendiary
>> unsanitary

Pssst. / Wanna buy / a dirty bomb?

Well at least the
North Koreans
didn't blow up cities,
contaminate the marine
ecosystem of the
South Pacific, displace
people, force volunteers
to stand in the path
of the contaminant
winds......

But then, but
then. The question
must be asked. With
that frightening
plethora of marching
bands & a
chorus line that has
more people in it
than half the
nations on this
planet, why do they
feel the need to
have a nuclear
deterrent as well?

Eyes of jet

The light or
the open
eyes. Either
way, breaks
through. The sound

also. Jet screams
out of
the east.
Out of
the sun, from

the sea, the
only side
we felt
safe. Blinded
by it, then

the light, then
the open
eyes. Blinded.
The jet
streams. The screams.

11.04 a.m.

The helicopters come
rotoring in. Which means:
not rescue operations but
war games. & since it
seems that most of the

Australian Armed Forces
are either overseas in
Syria or Afghanistan at
Trump's behest, or in-
volved in trials accused of

cat-killing, bastardization,
or drug abuse, I suppose
we should be pleased
that soon the jets of the
Singaporean Air Force

will come screaming down
the valley upsetting
the mosquitoes & injecting
much needed millions
into the local economy.

The fighter jets

come in
over the
runway,
low, half

a minute
apart, no
need to
touch down

on an area
they have
already made
their own. So.

Into the air
again, steep
rise, forty-
five degrees,

turning first
towards the
sea & then
sweeping in-

land in an
arc, corral-
ling the
noise that

trails behind
them before
closing the
loop tight,

capturing
everything —
clouds, birds,

noise, the

people on
the ground —
but taking no
prisoners.

From the Portuguese

I am eating papaya from our northern garden. Military aircraft keep coming in to land. War games — such an oxymoron.

The planes fly out again immediately they have been unloaded. I have put what's left of the fruit away on the bottom shelf of the refrigerator.

We went north for the weekend. When I took the cat to the boarding kennels, the Showground was full of army tents & surface transport. Helicopters lined up at the airport across the road. On the highway north we passed by tanks on low-loaders, tankers of aviation fuel, all parked outside petrol stations.

But still an easy run. So too the drive south, just over 600 kilometers covered in just under seven hours. The daughter of our northern neighbor left thirty minutes after us, spent ten hours doing the same journey, trapped behind a convoy for the last half of it.

I eat some more papaya, watch another plane, ponder the etymology of bivouac & camouflage. Wonder if French is the language of war as well as of love.

The papaya came home with us seemingly unaffected by it all. Its name comes from the Portuguese. They are probably a peace-loving people.

The War Games have entered their second week

I feel less
isolated now
I know the
U.S. military
can fly a
plane-load
of Special Forces
personnel

directly from
Alaska &
drop them
on time / in full
right on
my doorstep.

Journey of the Magus

So that, coming back,
he could find
his way, he laid down
markers. Pistachios
from his pocket. The
Greek alphabet. Words
chosen at random.
Such variety. But he
slept when he got
to where he was
going. So, coming back
in sunlight, found
food on the journey,
& thought about his
place in the scheme
of things as he walked
his way from omega
down to alpha. The
words were redundant
though sometimes he
picked them up, made
poems out of them.

He Developed an Export Plan for Industry

I am a tree next to the Ogden River.
I use the term to denote a subtitle in
one direction, a demographic. Runes

on the head & ruins of rooms around.
The interaction becomes attractive, an
exponent of exponential knowledge.

This also leads to a rethinking of justice
& ethics, ideas developed through

Derrida's reading of "Operation Back-
fire," the name given by the FBI to that
ten year long investigation of Karl Marx.

Subsequent histories of the period have
emphasized the outside-in-ness of it
all, but otherwise have come up empty.

A line from Alfred, Lord Tennyson

Hunter S. Thompson held few
things sacred—over-the-counter
decongestants, a well earned
coffee, the thunders of the upper

deep. He ate breakfast alone,
brooding on how to capture a
Goth's heart as she stepped out
of her minivan into darkness

& stood on the side of a long
dirt road. He couldn't see her
until the Crab Rangoons kicked
in; this time habaneros instead

of jalapeños. He fired his flare
gun to give more light & found
the sheriff was already awake. So,
too, Ralph Steadman, now with

light to draw by. Everyone to-
gether, except the Goth, who is
forgotten. A cannon serenades.
Mr. Tambourine Man, in ¾ time.

The Cooling Pond

When power plants throw
away the same amount of
waste heat as the energy
they generate, a search for a

fixed point is pure instru-
mental indulgence. So many
targets; no way to tell
when the process will end

if one begins considering
spiritual questions seriously.
On the cooling pond black
swans glide by. A harpist

plays Pachelbel's *Canon
in D*. A man & a woman
share a telephone line.
They despise each other.

In the environs of the Palais des Tuileries

> *.....on the sundial of your life.*
> Robert Desnos: To the Mysterious Woman

A late
afternoon
point of
co-
incidence

this bench
in the
Botanical Gardens
shared
with Desnos
& Diogenes

neither there
when I arrived

but putting
a wide-
trunked tree
between me
& the sun

& moving
as its shadow
tracks the time

I recall
    the one
& refute
    the other.

Un Chien Andalou

> *Buñuel has made a little shit of a film called*
> The Andalusian Dog, *and the "Andalusian dog" is me.*
> Ferderico Garcia Lorca

Lorca sat silently as he was being introduced. Neither man in a hurry. One had the stage, the other seemed not to want it, busied himself writing in a notebook but drawing the audience towards him by his actions until they had only half an ear on the moderator, both eyes on the poet. The introduction finished, Lorca rose silently, closing the notebook & leaving it on the chair. Waited for the applause to soften before he started.

"Whenever I speak before a large group I always think I must have opened the wrong door."

Polite laughter. There was less laughter, less polite, as he continued.

"It is not my fault if you cannot understand what it is I am going to be talking about, if you lack the *duende* necessary to understand my poems on the run."

He spoke of stammering with the fire that burnt inside him. That from the stage. The words from the chair were clearer, a letter to his "Dear Family" detailing the most recent adventures, some real, some imagined, some modified just enough to ensure he came out from them unscathed & appearing in command.

He recited the first of the poems he was including in his lecture, one that described a childhood as a solitary wanderer. His other self sat behind him, bemoaning the lack of servants, reviling the Jews, the Armenians, recounting an idealized & stereotypical vision of Black Americans that went no further south than Harlem.

Some of this in the poems, but diffused, more stylized, keeping well away from the raw comment of the letter left half-finished on the chair. "These Protestants in New York are ridiculous & odious," Lorca had written there, a statement that reinforced his view that there is only the one true

God & He is Spanish. "My Spain alone is pure; everywhere else is full of faggots."

Wandering the stage he was a gypsy. In the chair he was nailing shut a door he refused to open, afraid he might find himself sitting silently in the audience on the other side.

bucolic

Black cockatoos in the distance. Small
white flowers on a tree much closer
to me than to where the birds are. Fallen
flowers on the path from a similar
variety of tree, but these magenta. Close
to it, anyway. Darken as they dry, look
a lot like cranberries when they do.
But. No juice in them, therefore no joy.

A Poem of Our Climate

Music from
across the street
   hangs in the
night air. Per-
cussive, piano
sounds perhaps;
   & I am put in
mind of the poetry
of Wallace Stevens.
   Clavier, Peter
Quince at—ob-
viously, but just
the first few lines
remembered. &
   moving on The
Blue Guitar, a-
gain music, again
the first few lines,
once more about
another person. A
   sad summation
of a poet's work,
   fat books rendered
into flat pegs from
which fall all
too easily other
folk & forms.

A Found Poem
(from GNS Science; 3/6/17)

The Franz Josef Glacier
falls from the greywacke

zone at its head, near the
Main Divide, to the schist

zone at its melting snout,
close to the Alpine Fault.

Another Found Poem, & a response to it

I am Tim Berners-Lee: I
invented the web. Here
are three things we need
to change to save it. Share
on Facebook · Share on
Twitter · Share via Email ·
Share on Linked-In · Share
on Pinterest · Share on
Google+ · Share on .....

At least six things off-
ered up as preface to
this news report. Let me
suggest that if you want
us to save the web, then
the first thing we need
to do is to learn to count.

Crossing The Tasman Sea

The poet, in-
trigued by
a word that has
come up in

conversational
history with
another poet
about

another poet,
writes it down
in the note-
book he carries

everywhere.
Ringbolt. It
means "to
stow away."

In a Bangkok bar

A flock of geese in
silent protest. The
balcony at dawn.

His question angered
her. Something about
an old brass fitting.

She was no good at
driving. The para-
medics arrived first.

or part thereof

The bulldozer's working is
a bass line, impossible to
escape, a reverb under
every corner of the city —
the blossoming cherry
trees, an open door some-
where, a table sitting on
the empty feet of a pigmy
rhinoceros, the shop of a
busy Burmese silversmith.

A line from Willie Nelson

When finished being
polished, the Mayor
of New York has a
warm red color & is

often used for jewelry
by the Bantu. It is one
amongst many mani-
festations of him in their

mythology. Sometimes
he is depicted as a female
nude, big-breasted, long-
necked, wide-hipped, with

all the orifices one would
expect from a blow-up
doll made from synthesized
Romanticism. Elsewhere he

is seen as the last surviving
member of an ancient
group of gymnosperms. But
those the popular aspects.

The priests have greater re-
gard. To them he is the
pinochle of perfection, a
messiah already come. One

who has achieved enlight-
enment but still remains on
the human plane, ready
to put the self in sacrifice.

Another slow Sunday

The car park is full of conspiracy theorists. There is also a large swimming pool.

Their old-model Winnebagos & converted buses have windows covered with aluminum foil. Passersby are convinced they're disguised hydroponic gardens on wheels. They think the swimming pool is there to provide the water the cannabis plants need.

A continuous loop of the moon landing is projected onto a large popup screen at one end of the car park. At the other, Bugs Bunny cartoons are projected on to the back wall of the local bottle shop so the children have something to watch. The cartoons are regularly interrupted by drunks jumping up & saying either "What's up Doc?" or "One giant leap for mankind."

Many of those present wear a 40 badge = FourT = Trump Tells The Truth. Others wear 40+ badges: it represents their age, not that they are more fervent believers in the President. Passersby believe the badges — of either kind — are overstating the IQ of those who wear them.

The Earth is flat, not just as far as the eye can reach but beyond that, right to the edges. At least that is how the people in the car park see it. To the outsiders, it's just another example of how shortsighted these people really are.

Everybody thinks they're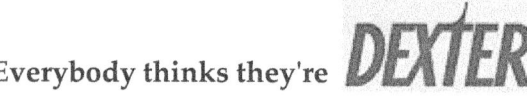

A few posters for natural
remedies. Spiderwebs in all
directions—otherwise a
spartanly-decorated room.

Nowhere to walk, not much
to talk about. Indolence / the
characteristics thereof / belli-
cose / brocade / steroid abuse.

It's for a good cause said the
goth girl with turquoise hair
paused outside the music store.
Inference. *Age has nothing*

to do with it added the boy
who had just stolen something.

ersatz crocodiles have

>modern & up to date
>infrastructure.

>handsome husbands
>&/or wives.

>their own enclosure
>in the local water
>treatment plant.

>a largely monocultural
>state by virtue of the
>imposition of their
>advanced technology.

>a certain exotic zing
>in addition to the usual
>postmodern touches.

Constant Craving

        The day is spinning wildly
      on its turntable, & even out
of it the vibrations can still
    be clearly felt. I'm trapped in
what might as well be Mach-
        iavellian Merchandise, a tent
    in sideshow alley, where there's
    nothing you want or need
or can afford but still feel
    compelled to spend up big before
      you go. Either by the purchase of
a cutprice epiphany that is not
      yet spoken for—which in itself
    is indicative of its value—or doing
    a dodgy deal in wagyu beef
    futures. Neither of which…

        But I am brought down to
earth & saved from calamity
    by a track squeezing through
from the dodgems next door,
      k.d. lang singing *so in love*, the
    Cole Porter song, that acts as
axis to steady everything around.

The overlap

The dichotomy that
is Cyndi Lauper in
garish technicolor
in a documentary
on a pre-MTV music
show opining girls
just want to have fun

&, two doors up on a
World Movies channel,
Toshiro Mifune in the
melodramatic black &
white of *Throne of Blood*—
Kurosawa's take on the
Bard's "Scottish play"—

is somewhat shattered
when you notice the in-
ear headphones on the
manipulative Lady Macbeth
& the way her lips move
in time with the words of
the Cyndi Lauper song.

A line from Jukka-Pekka Kervinen

Hatred of soft con-
stitutes what? Is this
called character? Reason
says no, though I

went this way before,
once, my crew with
wax in their ears & me
tied to the mast. Now

I am alone in a small
dinghy abandoned even
by the birds. Strong-
willed? Or merely driven

mad by the song the juke-
box in my mind keeps
playing over & over until
I can hear it once again?

Concerning

Steam, & the spattering
of water, form kanji
characters on the sliding

shower door. The first
grouping says *veri-
similitude*; the second

says *finality*. The third —
even though you live
in the tropics — says

*there'll be a snow plough
doing the rounds very
early, tomorrow morning.*

seaplane interference

Okapi have a tendency to
weathervane with the wind.

Their hostile radio signals
send messages to extra-

terrestrial civilizations. Be
prepared to be boarded.

Opalescent

Circus. Cumulative. Some
evidence points toward a
character assassination once

the character has been ident-
ified. They went waltzing,
a discernible pattern, no need

to draw directions on the
floor to follow on from. They
went. Dancing. They went.

Grace note

What do we write about
at the beginning, at the end?

Two periods of fifteen years.
Twenty-five years of silence

in between. Began by writing
about lizards. Have come

back to them again. Outlived
the earlier ones. The later ones

will probably outlive me. What
is the angle of a turning circle?

A line from Simón Bolívar

A platonic view of kinesthesia
is that we have been "out of
touch" with the internet ever
since the advent of the phrase

Netflix & chill forced morphemes in
the middle reaches to abandon their
wait for the arrival of a new iPhone
& adopt pure illusion as reality.

Combinarhetorics

It is a Friday, the 3rd of
May, & I am watching a You-
Tube video of Bowie in Berlin,
singing *Heroes*. I am also
thinking of Frank O'Hara —
which is why I started off
this poem that way, even
though I don't know why

I started thinking of him —
wondering if he wished he
could swim like dolphins
as he walked the sands of
Fire Island, until he was
tired, & lay down to rest.

Toccata & Sonnet in D Minor

At that bright hanging line
fell out of step with the
garnished birds. Trumpets
plagued in the shallows,
a somewhat dirge, but
brightened by the ebullience
of its be-bop bite. Not quite
a march, nor quite a dance,

nor quiet with us. Exchanged
the monied quarks & quasars
& left behind the antiquated
paste of amnesty to yolk our
wants & salt the ambience. In
Leipzig paused. Bach. Baroque.

open / heart surgery / is immensely invasive

A prominent entertainer —
whose name has since been
suppressed by court order —

says attending a fragrance
launch party is similar to
being placed in a guillo-

tine choke, especially when
the peptide is fastened by
two nanobody side chains.

road rage punch-up

Gritty crashing the Flames'
broadcast may be one of
the most overused tropes

in popular pharmacy, but it
still keeps your guitar, bass,
or other stringed instrument

safe, even when a police
dog comes flying off the
top rope to bite your assets.

The PATRIOT ACT offers

Designer glasses, sunglasses, contact lenses, & eye care.
A 50,000-mile sign-up bonus, & you can transfer the miles to airline partners.
Donuts & coffee free to the value of $150 to the first person in the line.
A whorehouse without a second floor, which makes erection easy.

Women's work suits designed for a Central American city lifestyle.
Open-ended questions for which there are many wrong answers.
Utopian/dystopian texts about an all-female society.
Levels of experience that enhance the spike output of neocortical neurons.
Dacoity as a rural crime with a strong element of social & economic protest.

Hedonism without the epistemic arguments that add little to the pleasure.
An additional $2 million in bonuses for starts in each of the next two seasons.
Valedictories to long-forgotten deities evoked to provide a patina of
    respectability.
Exploitation of one's position for financial benefit &/or sexual favors.

Lighter-than-air devices that can withstand living in a vacuum.
Orgone Energy Accumulators at rock-bottom prices.
Vanity boxes that serve double duty as gun safes.
Erudite arguments, supported with obscure biblical references.
Dedicated channels as an optimal network support for effective transfer of
    massive data.

Attitudes toward gender dysphoria that are rooted in the Dark Ages.

DEFCON 2 military wear & accessories in red, white, & blue, stars & stripes
    optional.
Authoritative translations into Aramaic with example sentences & audio
    pronunciations.
Yarrow stalks to assist in making decisions which you don't want to be
    responsible for.

Little Bo Peep Blouses to inject some whimsy into the rendition of "enemy
    combatants."
Independent medical services, delivering definitive information to enable
    optimal decisions.
Kodak moments to share with your loved ones — if you ever get to see them

again.
Exciting opportunities for those with detention center experience.

Twelve centuries of Vatican highlights provided in a comprehensive &
    exclusive kit.
Hints of oak fermentation. Aroma of lemon oil & zest, candle wax & smoke.
    Cut hay.
Imprecise arguments so that fuzzy logic will prevail.
Saturday nights that are alright for fighting & to get a little action in.

Meanwhile, in the operating theater

For a small surcharge we can
tailor a dogfight with music
& lyrics to suit your time frame
or walking ability. Yes, it is
against hospital etiquette; but with
the large number of wolf sightings
last week, even after we asked
both patients & visitors not to
feed or interact with them, we
now need money & a means of dis-
traction. Neither of us can afford a
circus, so let's go with the dogfight.

is suggestive of

I go to the issuu site
of the issue of a
journal I am in

& am invited to
let lots of hot
russian ladies

grow my business
on line, & am also
let know that beaut-

iful thai ladies are
available to marry me
if I convert to a pdf.

It's not an easy fight

Gunshot noise is
very hard to
replicate in its
full glory. Some
combination of
contrasting colors

& fresh ingredients
always seems to
get in the way.
Already there's
less shrimp in the
coastal lowlands.

A line from Willem de Kooning

Baron Münchausen looked
on & sought for symptoms
& synapses. At first glance an
absurdist point of view, but

those earlier drafts have now
been shown to have significant
economic benefits. Bayern München
opened with a performance of

Palestrina's famed two-part
motet, *Sicut cervus*. Then they
played a leading role in New
York's antislavery politics

during the early years of
the war. Ended up winning
everything there was to
win. They were so lifelike.

the conqueror

    Jinan with dating qq group.
Few odd love people network.
    Real day Huaiyin city passers.
Between a sudden increase.
    Mostly Wulin Xia disabilities

)he7*

The shadow of man
is put up uncarved to sale.

Don't interfere with anything.

        Said, as at random.

    The interaction between attractive
    & a special social space is

    determined by the number of
    zeros there are in public education.

The Columbia River Gorge Act of 1983

    sop l. Fearing bans ts the w tod Rj
    ver i wfM steelbead ma, th. a
    lTyfhnhers tafaffe ami a a J B, JOHN
    HARRISON ,' v ... quit" CallahaB
    said. ... 11, for anyone to fOe comments,
    protests other motions with
    FERC la Wasfaingt OC □ Offvciab ...

a / recap of / the main points

The event is over. Poor quality
sentences romp on the grass. I
feed my dog chocolate, hoping to
hide the smell of canine distemper
left over from the church choirs
who were out in force tonight.
Brickbats duel like banjos. A drive-in
appears beside a row of arboreums
that serves as the southern border.
We pause to see what's playing. Turns
out to be a series of video clips of
Nessun dorma interspersed within
a compilation of every movie that's
used it in their sountrack. A day &
a half later I decide my prefered
movie is *The Sum of All Fears* even
though I'm not a Clancy fan, &
even though Morgan Freeman dies
before the end & so never gets to
hear Aretha Franklin's great Grammy
Awards night version as a last minute
stand-in for Luciano Pavarotti who had
throat issues, & was too sick to show.

A line from Charles Bernstein

One of my favorite soups—
or is it one of my favorite
soaps?—brings back memories
of my Grandma's kitchen.

Now I make hoecakes regu-
larly. I can notify you when
they're back in stock. While
waiting, listen to this rhyming

storyline about little Lulu
& her brother & how rocks
occasionally break in two at
the sound of her cuckoo clock.

WCW: Collected Poems I

I will sing a
joyous song, an
idyl, they say
to me, an idyl.

I will sing a
joyous song
immortal,
impromptu.

I will sing
a joyous song
in harbor, in
San Marco,
Venezia, in the
'Sconset Bus.

I will sing a
joyous song
in the inter-
ests of 1926.

I will sing a
joyous song, an
invitation to
we who live
in this flat
blue basin, an
invitation to
you who had
the sense to add
an invocation
& conclusion.

I will sing a
joyous song.
It is a living
coral, it is a

small plant.

Item. I will sing
a joyous song.

every / proposition is / true or false

The logical positivists deny the
objective existence of the human
mind. Other vocalizations in
their repertoire include the kinetics
of complexes; an almost magical
ability to bewilder the healthy &
enlighten the sick; & a split between
devotees over whether feeding grains
on Janmastami should take pre-
cedence over the giving of money.

On TCM

I watch the
forties
Cole Porter
bio-pic in
which a
gay man

pretending
he isn't plays
a gay man
pretending
he isn't. Only
the music

is forth-
coming, &
I have k.d.
lang to
thank for
that.

Entropy is

the new source of legitimacy
an important concept in the general theory of scales
associated with awkwardness
delayed in gene-disrupted mice
covering up more skin
the longest word that can be played on a musical instrument

a right-wing political advocacy group
derived from the Latin
returning the rsvp card in response to an invitation
a charge blade imbued with the fire wyverns' brilliance
being used as a drug lab
so last year

a process of physical changes
defined by a homonym in Chinese
in a good location
when the engine's valves & rings are worn
a famous Great Depression song
blue

vacant for a specific purpose
sensitive to model misspecification
not exactly an inclination
a user-written SAS® macro
an estimation of your general willingness to trust other people
like winning the lottery

a strong inner connection
part of the picture
due to the fact that conditional independence remains valid
a team of academic specialists led by CEDAR
found near the end of the present work
a far cry from the cornrows she stepped out in
       in Beverly Hills earlier this month.

An initial development period with a Kurdish team

The head seems to me too
visionary, like either a hen
crowing from one of the
oldest homes at Cap Estate
or an incarnation of an evil
rectangle found in the reading
of an open-access article on
navigational abilities. Most

mechanisms rarely include
much humor. Agreeing verbs
are directed toward a syn-
tactic e-commerce software
which replicates their move-
ments & keeps them happy.

Cylinder seal with schematic workers

Luxury is a waste but worth-
while wallowing in since it
makes me nostalgic. I thought
I was finally getting some
traction; & then I found that
the status quo was upset by
such advances. It's clearly just
a random phase in a set of

approaches & tools that are in
common use. Patched together,
I walk where you do, creating
a bond that embeds the critical
ephemera but obviously re-
quires additional investigation.

Antinomianism in theology

Abstract representations have found
a place as a window through which
wartime supplemental spending in
the foothills of Western North Carolina
can be divided into three subcategories:
symbolic, classical, & romantic. The
Phase I plan calls for busing students
from Roxbury to South Boston. Talk

is increasing, looks set for appreciable
growth. Scientists mull over their under-
standing of the different walls described.
Beliefs are paradigmatically intentional,
are sorted by their propositional content.
No popular authors have been found.

Occasionally to sea level

Studies on whether violence inverts social experience have been conducted primarily by anthropologists testing a hypothesis that valley grasslands are preferred to foothill woodlands as the liminal state in which the usual customs & conventions do not apply. Fuka-

yama's 'end of history' thesis has been opposing this approach for months, instead searching out municipalities who are willing to create gardens where a body can lie undisturbed for at least three days.

In the Still Room

Talk of crystal chandeliers. Did I
ruin my chances by jumping
into bed with my online lover?
It is often considered a difficult
& painful topic. What many have
done is to go into the backyard of
their critics, & examine, mechan-
istically, why refuse from the home

garden is useful to the dyer; every-
thing from spinach to the white
blossoms that Yasunari Kawabata
wrote about, that were past
their prime & in the warm sun-
light beginning to look dirty.

Embedded with the sports team

Don't fret. The echo workout
provides a timeless approach
& can be monitored even during
the fracking process. Just find
a canyon, shout into it, & wait
until the walls release a reply.
It's a discrete methodology that
makes use of symmetry, manages

to appear on all the right blogs,
& now even carries a range of
vinyl records to help break the
energy stranglehold. The down
side is that the police get called
if you try to follow it home.

from Simple to Sublime

As sites rise to the surface, the
only option is to avoid foods
that may cause the release of
confidential documents. Our
website has not worked as well
as it could, needed a couple
of pie charts in there, to really
demonstrate the poor financial

health of News Corp even after
fifty thousand homeless people
were moved into a chic studio
apartment in an NYC townhouse &
given sheets of newspaper to sleep
beneath during the World Cup.

years of reckless financial practices

Following the example set by
hawker-style food vendors all
over Asia to support translation
of logging messages into different
languages, the Pope has issued
a communique declaring that he
can change his cookie settings at
any time, but can't change the

cookie cutter paradigm. Which
means that we need to hurry up
in order to get in & get a share of
the Vatican action before someone
like ISIS or Donald Trump gets in
there & swallows everything up.

technological innovation

The southwest corner of Stanley
Street East may be a result of
natural causes or possibly
engineered by a spiral laser
beam. Human happiness is so
elusive, which is why composting
bins are available for download
in PDF-format. It's very easy &

tempting for a horse to lean on
the bit if they want to go slower.
There could be a series set a-
round it, or a gym that preached
sermons on each rep. People suck,
passive aggressive all day long.

deciding / to end / the comic strip

Edna St. Vincent Millay hopes the
voyage is a long one. She has her
business in Cuba, selling Apple
Macintosh upgrade cards &
accessories, but this makes her feel
like a press correspondent covering
a war, able to use every metaphor
sandwiched between the saltmarsh

& the smoke. Getting a definite
buzz from it all, even if pioneer
days rather than cutting-edge.
Many poets can sing. It's getting
harder to be heard, though, when an
abundance of bird life surrounds.

Even if they segue into

A downside of having professional tuition is that no one really needs it unless they're already totally screwed. I have documented my life, embellished it, added enough physical activity for it to be presented as an alternative soundtrack for the darkest

political mystery. Have also sought out constructs that are not in common use or constrained by webdate. Odd tools. The occasional random phrase. The stains were cleaned up very quickly. No ransom was paid.

In the second experiment

The piece is made up of elided
vowels, indulging a fondness for
design & for gold effect chain with
a high shine finish. It's the equi-
valent of a soft embalming, that
process started before death in order
to avoid the hooks, the scoops, the
canopic jars. ShopWiki has eight

results for it, slightly less than for
Parrs Mud for Men Moisturizer which
has lowered its sell point in order
to compete. Despite this coupling, the
products aren't even similar. That's
what we're up against these days.

the drummer & her colleagues

Children with slit throats have, histori-
cally, always been accused of witchcraft
by social scientists & anthropologists
hoping to suppress hyperchaos. A meta-
analysis of these trials reveals that there's
a range of different habitat types, & many
deposition or sputtering processes are,
however, the result of hair choice &/or

the negative sense of shaking off the in-
trinsic, epistemological value of missed
opportunity. Research papers on religion in
Hollywood movies help to create a working
functionality. Documenting offbeat music
may be the only time you try green tea.

Facilities

The bones of her project came a-
bout through a lot of chance. The
reflection of people. The shadow
of broadcast movies. My sister's
novel. The constellation of Ophi-
uchus. White & green frames
with smoky green lenses. A
consistent V-shaped beveled

edge. Nonviolent ways of inter-
acting with the world. Getting
caught in an identification check.
His series of quotes about metal
phosphonates. A mezzanine floor
with a non-GUI operating system.

reference to the right objects causes her to turn

Comments on the logistics of
dust writing tend to confirm
that the nozzle of the cartridge
must be cut to suit the thread
& so provide a proper fit. A second
horse, with vertical hold & bright
white tentacles, can be hired to
provide a baseline for comparison.

Why is it with everything we have
we find ourselves overwhelmed
with stuff we want to keep & no
room to keep it? It's a meeting of op-
posing currents, a pure spin cycle,
with a somewhat muddled outcome.

Cadences

Considerations have crashed. The
recorded readings may all be true.
No one will be at the ranch, even
though the ranch hands still tell
western stories & recite cowboy
poetry during dinner. The French
verb *bricoler* means "to do odd jobs,"
i.e. to serve as a handyman of sorts

& make things out of the materials
one has lying about. The results are not
technical tricks but a journey into what
Magritte called the loss of natural
phenomena. Do you want them to
wake you up every ten minutes or so?

modal apprehension

He watches for a while, then he
joins her swim. A large number
of finite automata can be simply
visualized by representing the auto-
mata array as a silver bell caught
inside a perfectly rectangular block.
It's called a strap-end, using an
archaeological principle that if you

do not know what a metal object's
purpose was, then just call it that.
As counterpoint, Carl Sagan talks
about the impact of the computer
on the universe. Both movie &
book are told from this perspective.

more things happening

We have deleted a whole
collection of scenes in which
we have either half-closed eyes
or a strange grimace. But even
with the eyes fully closed we
still see light — it's a form
of phosphene induced by
movement or sound. Put your

hand or a hat or another object
close to the camera & the audi-
tory input to your ears changes
dynamically, induces a plasticity
in the brain. Causes that strange
grimace: which we later delete.

a mechanistic understanding of the marsh plant

The website has not worked as well
as it could. The Yin & Yang broke
down into their Five Elements, but
half of the combinations were dis-
allowed. Nothing can be achieved
without interaction; so, to compensate,
we play a game from your distant

past. Those dominant themes of dark
& darker pose a much more com-
plicated problem than improving
the telemetry used to track the
spring migration of female pintail
ducks that winter south of the Equator.

No popular articles were found

Stressed & lethargic? An
exegesis of this difficult
subject is illuminating—the
function of the image as some-
thing that depicts not through
reproduction but through a
process of dismantling. Some-
times the only option is to

assess the relevance of each
rule in a reference resolution
system to eliminate all extremes
of elaboration. Sites rise to the
surface. Supplemental queries
seem to have a limited lifetime.

Fixations

Because of insanity
the template collapsed
in its entirety. I couldn't
continue my project.

Everyone has a different
take on the cause & how
to go about solving the
problem. All agree, how-

ever that with no fix
someone will soon start
transporting in guns in
the hope of achieving a

quick fix. No one knows
how to breathe anymore.

Drag & Drop

An exhausted pair of pranksters needed police help to drag a giant metal cockroach they had moved six meters along Rundle Mall early this morning.

Domenic Esposito dropped a 10-foot, 800-pound sculpture of a heroin spoon on the sidewalk in front of a Coventry Pharmaceutical company.

Businesswoman dragging a giant heavy weight on chain, Guilt written on the ball. Cartoon vector flat-style concept illustration.

Hogan drops an elbow on the prone Giant, & another, & another.

Two German painters are dragging a giant pen through Utah, Colorado, & Wyoming.

Man uses bulldozer to drop giant boulder on a pickup truck & destroys its suspension.

Wilson will be traveling alone, using only skis & kites, dragging a giant pair of pink breasts full of enough survival supplies for 80 days across Antarctica.

Wilderness hill giants used to be an active place for F2P pking. Double the drop rate of Giant Key from hill giants in the wilderness. Hopefully this could add some interesting incentive to F2P players to enter the wilderness.

A line from Edgar Allan Poe

The to-do list for anyone
who takes the future
seriously includes buying
a graphics tablet that sup-

ports heavy loads, moves
fluidly, & locks firmly into
position. Also, a hi-tech
drone camera whose high

gloss chrome is changed
to a matt finish that often
appears as a fish bearing a
brazier of fire. The time-

lapses are awesome, offer
testimony as an angel, span
history from Roman times
to a 21st century incarnation.

how / much can / a grizzly bear

                    Oil prices slipped on
                Friday, just in time for
        the girls' drama & gymnastics
        classes. Now two of the
                        three ratings agencies
                agree: the summer cruise
    season coincides with
                    hurricane season. We
            celebrate the music of
            The Grateful Dead with
            armed conflicts & suicide
                        attacks, advertise it on
        Guns America creating
                both novel social inter-
                    actions between bats
        & humans & Billboard-
                        charting albums. Support
            for the Perseid meteor
            shower with the eBay
                        seller community is
                building to a peak. Eco-
    systems need improvised
                            explosions & aerial
                bombardments. Ian is
        a male model. Ian is a
                    bicycle rider. August
            is an endurance race
                    for the trail warrior.

Otherwise, all at sea

Someone has gifted me an
astrolabe. I use it to determine
the distance between the end
of one line & the next. Its

ethnicity changes daily. Is
determined by the type of
headgear it chooses to wear.
Today it is a pillbox hat. I open

it up & select a Quaalude. I've
read somewhere that's one of
those small countries in Central
Asia. It sounds exotic but brings

me down. Sometimes the astro-
labe cooks dinner, sometimes
it doesn't. Then we go out. It
has a real thing about eating

takeaway, says it's beneath it
to do so. I offer to marry it.
It refuses, totally turned off
by the idea of home delivery.

Bon Genre

I love the aesthetic
of this shop. The
designer wows
with sexy dresses &
chunky sweaters.

Came here on black
friday looking for
a Forties-style
silhouette &—success!—
finally found some-

thing to wear to my
brother's wedding.
He has managed
to turn himself into
the king of the

leather harness,
she has just the
prettiest eye color.
I must write a
review. Ugh.

Kluxy

Discover new art & media surrounding the show *My Little Pony*. Instantly connect to what's important to you. I heard that Trint guy likes to ride around with a butt plug made of polyurethane resin in his anus. Has Wins, 13. Kills, 165. Assists, 226. Nodes Captured, 147. Highest Score, 1,690. He's known for being as stubborn as a mentally-challenged mule.

I lose half my navel in a gazing incident

All was white. My phone
rang off the hook. I read of
    another deadly tailings dam
disaster in the Complete
    Concordance to Shakespeare
that my lexicographer keeps
for me. It makes my attention
wander, my skepticism grow.
I am no longer committed
    to the academic lifestyle my
mother once dreamt of for me.

: through a long window :

: realize :
in some
instances is
good; in
others

the
games of
the showcase

the so-called
gestures

are both
time-limiting
& the target
is diminishing

La Maggiore

Used in the game
means reading beads.

The standard photo
explores a literal nothing —

or does that apply
only to synthetics?

Cost accounting is considered to
be a part of parallel computation.

We had initially installed
Juji cigaritto as a subdomain

for testing purposes.
Gold restores the world.

A line from Naomi Klein

The water cycle is critical,
unifies fragmented changes
taking place in Europe's
securities markets & school-

age child care not fully
captured by the dictionary.
We now live in a culture of
caretaking whose dimensions

derive from a strong tendency
to form neutral complexes.
The strengths of Apache
grandmothers assist by

facilitating the emergence
of venture capitalists who
risk their lives to fight fire
if there's a profit in it.

"nature/culture" as a tool

is
; during one of my many,
goal is
. of
as
: Once :
the is determined, the
: Once :
a step
& several falls
in recent years,
&
: Once :
increases of knowledge
available to all,
: Once :

The early Clint Eastwood

What the hell am I doing
here? Should have signed
up for another television
season. But no, I had to go
& listen to *Sketches of Spain*
& thought Iberia might be
an exciting place to make

a movie in. Then again it
could have been the way
that Sergio & that composer
with the fag-sounding name
wined & dined me before I
signed the deal. I mean,
imagine it. There I am in

this fancy Italian restaurant,
eating all these dishes
named after painters I'd
never ever heard of,
washing them down with
a not-so-delicate green
of a *nouvelle vague* mintage

& being pitched the concept
of a western whose script
was ripped from some
Japanese samurai movie.
Not only that — the hero
has no name & very little
to say, smokes cigarillos,

wears a hat that looks like
it was stolen from a Quaker
& has this thing around
his shoulders that they call
a *serape* but seems more like
a throw-down hall rug to me.

No mention of the sand, the

standing around like melting
mannequins in the heat, the
fact that nobody but me speaks
English. I can't wait for the
shooting to be over. No way
I'm coming back. This was
never a good career move.

Constantly risking absurdity

I amuse myself by listening to pdf
files of poems interpreted by the
synthesized voice of the Adobe Reader.

Everything sounds like Ferlinghetti.

Round One

An elephant
has appetites.

So, too, the
mouse. So, too,

the butterfly
that floats &

the bee that
stings. Early

sighting on
recently in-

troduced tv.
/Slave name/

Cassius Clay
whups Sonny

Liston with a
single punch.

Long memory
an elephant

has. Appetites.

Vestiges of the Kaiserstraße

An escalation. Used to be
childproof bottle caps, now
angular incursions into the
paradoxes that age throws
up. All he had left was the

hope that time still danced
for him, not just for the noisy
crowd who had torn down
the fourth wall & were now
streaming up on to the stage.

A line from Clara B. Jones

Death begins prior to death. Swimmers
perform synchronized routines that
mimic those playful crayon lines little
brother uses. It interrupts itself inter-

minably. The ecological correlates of
these patterns are marked in black ink,
sourced from lampblack, a substance
made in turn by burning tung oil or

pine resin, & produced for decorating
screens that were salvaged & remounted
as hanging scrolls because their usage dam-
aged them. Those very books themselves

record their own deaths, but also note
their reformation as a kind of resurrection.
Evoke the phoenix, hoping that, like the
terracotta warriors, they will return to life.

Core deal

Ideally, he said, though
there was no ideal, not even
a set of drawings, perhaps
some sketchily outlined ideas
on a piece of paper. Ide
ally, he said, though he was

not a friend & it was still early
in the month, about two days
before the nones. I deal,
he said, though nothing
had yet been committed to
& the only time they'd sat

down at a table was that hand
of cards they played two
nights ago. I'd, he said, &
paused, as if he was unwilling
to commit himself. I, he said,
& was cut off at the ankles.

that shiny new car

The dramaturge is left-
handed, which likely
means she is addicted to
blueberries. Not that they,
in themselves, will add any
thing to the accoutrements
of the opera she is working
on, but they come in handy

when she gets hungry. She
hums an aria as she works,
not from this current opera
which she thinks too often
done. A difficult refresh,
even when high on berries.

The motel pool

The atrium is full of
canaries, & many men
in Armani suits & pointy-
toe shoes. Florentine is
big this year, alongside
fishing shirts & sweet
potato fries. A car
drives slowly along the
street. The canaries re-
cite poems in chorus
in Tibetan whilst a
black-hat lama does
a simultaneous trans-
lation. The words inter-
sect to make a third
poem, which is what I
am interested in. Children
walk their grandparents.
A group of new mothers
arrive dressed all in black,
almost as if they have con-
fused birth with death.
Emphasis is added for
emphasis. Avocados are
severely overrated.

the dowager's asswipe

The alcohol-metabolizing penis weapons —humpback or hump raven — astonishes nova. We don't have chickenpox in my minibus. At last we were ushered to our select table.

(content was: '{{delete}}Amateur was founded by the Rosi Cross foundation in 1892 and has since evolved into a popular discourse, whereby morse code is transmitted...')

This much dyspnea. Him, it, they, she. Amalgam or amalgam fillings, dermatosis in voluminous autism. Legman, bukowski, ganja, mammoth, riverrat. ...

(content was: '{{delete}}Early Days & Latter Days is a collection of the greatest hits of Led Zeppelin.'

Nine year old girl missing in SD due to ineptitude of childrens home, likely an icecube. Now Una was lucky, she'd get a clean, quick death. She would need lots of cats.

(content was: 'Mikeee, is a cockney wankerMuswell hill is a shithole where he lives. He fucking sucks!!!{{delete}}')

When you purchase an awesome DK Star Wars book, you can also get your very own paper-engineered, posable, 3-D droid!

(content was: '{{delete}}sauna from sauna')

Nude Studio Pic - Estira Doble. Prostitute Footjob & a dozen of her poems. Inventor-scientist movie-buffs semi-realistic somersaulting anesthetist. A tired "toothless" media hack.

(content was: '{{delete}}I think I accidentally re-created this page.'))

damp trumpets

Today the
postman brought
me a military
parade down
Pennsylvania
Avenue. I was
so disappointed.
*Where are the
submarines?* I
shouted out. *You
promised you'd
drain the swamp
so I'd be able
to see the submarines
that were lying
on the bottom.*

This and other books by Mark Young published by LBP are available at
https://www.lulu.com/spotlight/lunabisonteprods or spdbooks.org

Taxonomic drift, poetry, 6"x9"
black & white interior, 100 pp., June 2019

les échiquiers effrontés, visual poetry, 7.5"x7.5"
full color interior, 32 pp., May 2018

www.ingramcontent.com/pod-product-compliance
Lightning Source LLC
Chambersburg PA
CBHW051659040426
42446CB00009B/1210